"Lyrical Freedoms from the Heart"

By
De'Vonna Bentley-Pittman
&
A Few Important People

"Lyrical Freedoms from the Heart"
By De'Vonna Bentley-Pittman
&
A Few Important People
Copyright © 2015 by De'Vonna Bentley-Pittman

Written and published by
De'Vonna Bentley-Pittman
www.devonnapittman.com
Minneapolis, MN 55411

Printed in the United States

ISBN 13: 9781512211818
ISBN 10: 1512211818

Author Photos by: Jay Kelly @ www.jaykellyimages.com
Cover Design by: Teóna Washington @ Toysun Enterprises

This collection is dedicated to all of those who have much to say, but don't yet have the courage to say it. Until you are able to speak up we will be your voice! These spoken words, poetry, and rants encompass our most deepest and most powerful emotions, opinions, and thoughts. They are our profound lyrics of freedom!

Prologue: Ten and a Half Commandments

No other gods before me

No graven images

Don't take the Lord's name in vain

Remember the Sabbath

Honor thy father and thy mother

Thou shalt not ....

Kill, steal, commit adultery, bear false witness

NOR covet!

Did Moses forget one?

Is it only a sin, if it's one of the 10?

The world will love you to life.

Make you feel like a woman

A grown woman!

Embellish you, and entrance you

Make you feel like you are somebody

Hold you tight

And whisper sweet nothings in your ear

But through it all, does love really conquer all?

Sunday after Sunday, "Love thy neighbor."

And, in the same breath

"Everybody aint gon' be yo friend."

"Feed em with a long handled spoon."

"Kill em wit kindness."

But, what does that really mean?

If Christ loved us why do we love less?

Is it only a sin, if it's one of the TEN?

The subconscious sinful nature

Constantly pulling, and overriding systems

Speaking with the tongues of men

And of angels

Without sincere love

Resulting in sounds of brass and clanging cymbal.

Moving forward without rendering yourself

Or trusting that He will rid you of yourself.

First love.

Share it with the world
Edify the masses
Unleash your first love
The world suffers without it
Not yours to keep
You were born to share it
Born with gifts and talents
To bring a world to repentance
Not to hide jewels in the sand
Or treasures in concrete boxes
Nor neglect the gifts bestowed upon us
Your gift was meant to restore us
To change a life, a world, a destiny
Yet you failed to share it
A world unrepentant
Wanting, needing
Lacking your gifts and talents
Unleash your first love upon all the earth
We need to experience it, rest in it
We need to be healed
Slow death we all die
For your gift was meant to save us
Invigorate your first love
Say yes, I do, I will
'I remember my first love'
Then walk in freedom and forgiveness
The unrepentant are waiting...
I decree it, share it, free it
To the world
Your first love
We are all waiting.

Strongholds

"Each of us has an invisible fence of sorts; we are struggling to get over or around it. Let us reach upward and climb over it with our bare hands, and whilst we are climbing, let us grab the hand of someone else."

Where is thy soul?

Somewhere between reality and fiction
Lies an unsettled soul
A powerful force
Bringing harmony to the world
So then, what becomes of the soul
Conceived in love?
And power, and sin?
A soul that lies between
Reality and fiction
Where love once ruled
What becomes of the seed of sin
And of love, and of power?
Conceived in love, and sin
By two powerful and beautiful souls
And, how can something be dark
And beautiful at the same time?
And then, create something
Destined to create harmony?
Bound together
By magnetism
That couldn't be defied
Love, and sin
And, two beautiful souls...
Conceived in the midst of love
Power, strongholds
And sin
What becomes of the soul
Conceived in sin?
And in power, and in love?
A soul that is full of greatness
Love, faith, and destiny!

Don't Tarry

"Don't tarry too long," I recall Bishop Frazier saying to children blocking a doorway at church. People, don't let ANY circumstance stop you from moving forward! Nothing is worth missing your destiny. If you knew my story, you would understand. The evident parts are that I dropped out of high school, had two babies by the time I was twenty, went back and got my diploma, and then I graduated from college. And, the rest is history. So, I say to you, don't tarry too long. Keep moving forward and don't let anyone, anything, any moment hinder your path!"

Crazy Lady

There's a crazy lady who lives inside me
Been there long as I can remember
In her own matter-a-fact way
Waiting patiently to speak
She's not your regular church member
She's walking in intellect and wisdom
Breaking down my own personal systems
Every twenty-something days
She comes and takes residence
Sensitive, yet profoundly prophetic
Sends chills up my spine
Taking precedence
Through the aches and pains
She brings retribution and infliction
Speaking to my mind healing and restoration
Once a month she takes control of my emotions
Hands me a mirror
And places me under subjection
Able to see my own reflection
Without selfish interjections
Sit down! Says the crazy lady
It's time for me to talk
Time for you to listen!
Nothing quite as profound
As her discerning intuition
Cramps overtaking my brain
And, my need to reason
This is the only moment I'm forced to listen
Better believe
I pay close attention

Strive!

"People often lose their passion and fire after years of being *saved* or religious, and need to find their way back to their first love. Sometimes that's not always easy. This can happen slowly or it can happen suddenly. We can become religious and allow church to become a routine. When we do that, it leaves room for mediocrity. God's looking for the "strive" in us!"

A Profound Misunderstanding

What did you just say?
I don't necessarily believe any of that.
Your eyes don't agree with the words you speak.
That laugh cascading like rippling waves
As it floats from your lips.
Entranced from the deepest chambers of your heart.
By the way, did you know your heart is divided
Into four chambers?
Two upper and two lower?
Yeah, that's all me.
Passing through your heart
Like ruby red oxygen rich blood.
Pumping, and flowing!
Yes, I'm responsible for all of that.
When I walk into a room, you fall in love with me
All over again...
I've uncovered a profound misunderstanding.
And now I have an understanding
Of what's not been understood.
I know you love the very essence of me
The very *idea* of me.
You love my mind, my sensuality,
My beauty, my finesse.
If you were God
I would have been created just the way I am.
Yet, there is a profound misunderstanding.
Now, with a profound understanding
You are no longer misunderstood.
Truth is...
The mystery wasn't so profound after all.

True Empathy

"When people say, "I'm just glad it wasn't my child
or my mother or my father." It's insensitive! It's
insensitive to those who ARE affected by tragedy or
loss. Mourn selflessly. Mourn with those who
mourn!"

Church Lady

Saints, be careful of your ways!

Yes, mam and yes sir, I said it.

Sinners got a song too

Souls waiting to be ministered to

Souls aching, but waiting

Decaying...

Asking questions

Getting half answers

Unofficial detectives in waiting

Missing opportunities

For healing and declaring

Head held high

Oblivious, and prospering

The call you're missing

While sinners are dying

Failing to hear

And, still you aren't listening

Yet, you are without sin,

In the lion's den

Judgement awaiting

What is the truth?

The question is, *who* is the truth?

Who among us has never sinned?

Therefore no condemnation?

Feeding off the power

Of sinful enslavement.

Have I sinned?

Did I do it?

Was I guilty?

Maybe!

But, you Mam...

You won't draw anyone

If you're a judgmental church lady!

You? The Antagonist?

"If they are still talking

And, you are still listening,

you…are one of them!"

Love's Epiphany

"What is this that's happened to me?
My heart, my mind
Wrapped up in epiphanies
So deep, so complex
Previously hidden within me.
From my core, the fibers;
Each of them fulfilled by this thing.
Connecting to me
In a way that had become foreign."

Native Treasure

Afro run free! Run free!
Overtake the reminiscent
Caribbean breeze
For a moment forgotten
No longer seeking to appease
Flowing in sync
With your very own nature
Finally bringing peace
To the earth's equator
Native pleasures, oh so divine
We give thanks
And praise to Thine
Most Holy God
For creating natural beauty
Raised my hand
And accepted my duty
Once confused
Heart and mind now clear
Proudly standing, embracing
And refusing to adhere
Shoulders held high
Delivering shameful vanity
Turning heads, thoughts
And securing my sanity
Ghana, Nigeria, Congo
Boasting of drums
Rhythms, and the bongo
Ivory Coast's distinct
Trait of curls and coils
The land that breeds
The nation's most precious oils
Togo, screaming!

13

From the depths of my being
Inherited a native treasure
Time to accept divine healing
You know the story
The crown I wear is my glory
Abracadabra...
Toe to toe in a mirror I stand
Nose to nose, honoring my native land
Two hundred and forty-five years later
Face to face with a reflective vindicator
Not from Australia or Alaska
From the deep, dark soils of Africa
Fertile with cocoa, timber, and gold
From her, I inherited
A treasure untold
Reflection standing before me
The queen I was meant to be
Thick, coily, wooly
Tight, dark, and curly
African Queen indeed!
Demanding to be free!
Running deep within me
Run free Afro, run free!

#Conquerors!

'I sometimes have to remind myself that I am ready. What I'm supposed to do, I am qualified and capable to do it! Who I'm supposed to be, I am becoming. He qualified me! Because God has dominion over all things, He has me. I'm no longer worried, my life is in His hands!'

The Box I Dread

There's a box in my house, up my stairs, under my bed, shoved so far that I have to nearly place myself under the bed to reach it. It lies there undisturbed and out of sight for several reasons. Mainly, because it holds things that are dear to my heart. Things that take me to a place in time that breaks me down to my core. I dread seeing this box because it is magnetic, it pulls me in whenever I get a glimpse of it. And, so I shove it far away. Today, I opened that box and two hours later I realized I was still digging through that box. I hadn't finished the day's chores, I had lost track of time and things were left undone. This always happened, every time I've opened the "dreaded" box. That *box* holds memories of people who greatly impacted my life; my uncle Jimmy, Aunt Carmella, Cousin Duna, Big Mama and Big Daddy, Grandma Sug, Mozzella Smith, Daddy George, Uncle Sam, and others who have gone on home to be with the Lord. Art from my children's kindergarten years brought back memories of their days of innocence, times I miss. By the time I closed the box several hours had passed by, but I hoped the next time would come sooner. In fact, I was almost sure that it wouldn't be long before I was shoving my body back under my bed to reach for that which has made me who I am.

Let God be God!

People who escaped the wrath of God kill me! Raining on someone else's mercy and grace! Talking about "what's done in the dark will come to the light!" When they ought to be glad the light didn't shine on their plight. What would we have seen? What should we have seen? The judgement is God's, Let God be God.

Check your pulse

"'I've learned that until you celebrate the successes of others, your success will truly never be celebratory. If something good or big happens to someone else, check your pulse. If you almost passed out because you were happy for them, Amen! If you almost passed out because you were jealous of them, take it to the alter!"

Beloved, I wish above all things that thou mayest prosper and be in health, even as thy soul prospereth.

3 John 1:2

What about ME?

In the process of loving you
I chose not to love ME
Sometimes introverted
And sometimes extraverted, ME
Quirks and all the PERKS of ME
I gave you ME!
While you were satisfied, full, and complete
ME got the short end of the stick
In the process of loving you
I put some things aside
Decided you deserved the best
And all life had to offer
So, I gave you what you wanted
I gave you ME
Gave you glitz, glamour,
My heart, mind and soul
Whatever you wanted
Whatever you needed
You need not even ask
I gave you ME
Put some dreams on hold
Friendships on hold
Love, on hold
Put ME on a platter
So, you could *have*...
Everything you ever needed
Handed it over without ransom
Without qualification, without multiplication
You see, one plus one equals two
Take ME out of the equation and you got one
One selfish, narcissistic, self-centered one
My heart?

Offering vulnerability
In its truest of forms
While ME waited on the sideline
For a fairy tale to come
ME waited on that once in a life time, kind of love
Butterflies in my stomach, kind of love
Can't sleep at night for thinking about you
Kind of love
Selling myself short
Falling for promise after promise
Broken like tempered glass
Crashing to the ground, kind of love
But, that was before love came in
And, stole ME away…
So, I stand here today to apologize to ME
And to say that from this day forward
I will put ME first!

The answer is NO!

'So excited about my blessing that I eagerly said yes. But, "God said...NO, that aint it, give it back!" WHAT Lord? "I said give it back, because I have something better for you. Something, just for you". Hesitantly, I replied, Okay, Lord I will await your call, patiently, without worry, anger or distress.'

Lord, I'm still waiting.

Mentee Turned Mentor

Let us never be the kind of mentor

Who envies the mentee

When they become the mentor

Let us praise and honor those we've spoken life into

Celebrate those we've breathed life into

Admonish the ones we fed in our kitchens

Bless those we've sowed financially unto

Let us praise the flowers we've watered

When they didn't know their roots were dry

Honor your mentee turned mentor

Do not be deceived by what is in your heart

Combat evil feelings with love

Respect, and adoration

Celebrate the mentor

Whom you once referred to

As beloved mentee.

"Pass Me Back My Load..."

Anointed, appointed, and called for a purpose
Testifying all over the world
Geared with a spiritual compass
Shining the light on the elephant in the room
Edifying survivors to move far from the gloom
Stop the façade, let down your guard today
Move from hurt and pain, I say!
For the enemy's job is to inhibit
To cast upon you unsolicited shame
To keep us bound by a dark and dangerous spirit
In the meantime, I'm casting down
And dispelling curses
Using lyrical freedoms
Delivering healing through verses
Declaring infallible promises of a great kingdom
Imploring each of you to walk in liberation
And freedom
Shall never forget the day I met a
unique woman...
Bound AND shackled
In her own personal prison
Confidently *walked*
But had a spiritual limp in her stride
Barely saw it until I tuned in and opened my eyes
Looked a little deeper
And innately recognized that spirit
Reminded me that there were still so many of us
Who suffer in silence
Not accepting that for her
There already had been recompense
Acoustic vibrations, *concoctic* relation-Ships
Passing in the night, not understanding my plight

Nor, why I was so forthright
Bore her soul, shed tears, and told me her story
Went line by line, while I took inventory
"Been hurt, abused, beaten
And boy do I got problems
They told me about a man who can solve em'
Know I need healin'
But, can't associate myself with that kind of somethin'
I ain't that common, you see I came from nothing
I'd rather carry this heavy load my sister, so let me be
After we done talkin'
I gets to go back to my own reality
Smilin', prosperin', and puttin' on a good ole' front
for the world to see
Past hidden six feet deep
Beneath my accomplishments
You see, my future is too bright
To chance losing my confidence!
Past too damn painful, ungraceful
Plain ole' shameful
Where was my arch angel?
So, for a second I'm laying it all on you
Don't believe there's nothing
A man name Jesus can do
Child, I ain't never told nobody
The things I'm telling you
I don't want a breakthrough
Not right now, not yet!
I got things on my calendar
Gonna see folks I never met"
"I hear what you sayin', I believe I can be free
But, not yet, I'm workin' on me!
No, I think I'll secretly carry this load
I'll weep from my soul

Feelings constantly hurtin'
True countenance hidden
Dark and solemn...
Livin' in my own world
A private microcosm
But, let me get going
fo' folks see us talkin'
And think I have problems
Wouldn't dare tell the world what I suffered
While my soul was being ruptured
Trying to smile involuntarily
Giddy, hurtin'
Often filled with sadness and pity
Truth is, I'm suffocatin' from all this weight
Though, six feet deep I buried all the hate
Won't allow my bright future to suffer
From a past filled with dark fate
I got places to go
Can't let anyone know about my death blow
But, you...you can relate
But, you...I can't emulate!
So, please don't make me late
Thanks for listening
I'll *never* forget you
You keep up the good ole fight
You get justice
For you reminded me
There's a Savior who can heal us
From all this slough, this stuff
Stuff we buried...six feet deep
Well...I best get goin'
C'mon give it to me...
Pass me back my load
It's mine alone to bear

I'm confidently walking away
Still limping
Before anyone notices me here…"

Spiritual Warfare of Domestic Violence

"It is the enemy's job to keep us bound and stuck.
When we are stuck we emit an aroma of low self-esteem and weak spiritual strength.
If we remain stuck, our community suffers
And our youth suffer.
Domestic abuse is a ploy from the enemy, and an abuser is a slave to the enemy.
Anything contradictory to what God commands is a clear indication that the actions are not of God, and are in total disobedience to the directives to love.
Think about this for a moment..
If I'm constricting you and discouraging you from being great
I am in the way!
If I can't visualize you greater next week, next month, next year, five, ten, fifteen years from now!
I am in the way!
Ultimately, if I love you, I want you to be all that God created you to be.
I need you to find you!
AND....If I'm not assisting
In the cultivation of your evolution,
I am in the way!
Victims of domestic abuse must seek help
Health and freedom
Be healthy in YOUR mind,
Be healthy in your heart, and your spirit!
At breakfast with my friend Ms. Tara Stone last week, she spoke wisdom from her soul, "Your freedom is not contingent on other people's opinions".
We must get this!

As long as you are unhealthy and tied to individuals who cannot love you the way God loves you, your growth will be stunted.

You cannot be who God called you to be when you're in pain, turmoil, and *constriction*.

Anything that is contrary to the love of God is not of God, and wars against our spirit and our destiny.

Find yourself, find peace.

Be free!"

Prioritize!

"We must prepare our children to compete. If it means sacrificing the things we love (such as shoes, purses, clothes) to pay for quality tutoring services, then we must do that. If you don't make those sacrifices for your children, it will be evident later. If our angels are not prepared, our communities suffer. Believe it now, or witness it later!"

A Father's Love

Though he never talked much, he provided for me. Though he never looked into my eyes, he showed me how to have integrity. He silently praised me when I did well. He cooked, cleaned and went to work every day. He earned a good, decent living and retired after working for the same company for over twenty years. Though, I didn't hear him say it, I knew it. Today I called him to tell him how much I love him and how much of a better person he made me. I completely adore him for being a REAL man when my own father walked away and completely forgot that I was even born. This man, my stepfather, John Isom has been a GREAT father. Not just to my siblings, but to ME! That man is to be praised. I called him to tell him all those things, and as usual he reminded me that he loves me too, and that he never misses a day thinking of me and my children or my husband. He said he's proud of me, and he was just looking at all the pictures that my sister sent him. He knows what I'm doing, he knows my husband, and he knows my children. He has not lost touch with who I am because, he is my father. I didn't want him to leave this earth without knowing how much I love, admire, and appreciate him. NOW, he knows that I love him. Now, he knows I remember his sacrifices. He knows how much he reminds me of the man I married, and most of all he knows that he's in my heart and his work was not in vain. He is my father.

Prelude: Ten and a Half Commandments

"I was asked to present a spoken word piece tonight at the *Minnesota AIDS project's Dialogue and Panel with Clergy*. The piece I performed is titled "Ten and a Half Commandments". Church folk, we must change that! There has got to be a place of solitude. If people don't feel loved in the church, they will find love somewhere else, anywhere else. One thing that stood out was that there has been much advancement including four one-a-day treatments that actually create healthier and longer lives for those affected. Once people who are infected take the meds it lessens the risk of exposure. Last, but not least GET TESTED!"

Upward Bound Together

Anyone can change
We can't hold people
To what they used to be
So, we have to allow them a clean slate
A chance to grow, evolve
And ultimately change
But first, we must consider ourselves
And, the equivalence of our own role
And how important it is
In the transformation of others
We are all moving parts
We are critical to the change
We want to see in others
We have to be the true examples
In love, be doers of the word
Not just busy preaching the word
Allow people time to prove themselves
In essence, we are proving ourselves.

When hurt, hurts!

"Our little hearts fool us to carry expectations that people sometimes simply can't meet. These are often expectations that they will never be able to meet. When we place even the most mediocre expectations on individuals who don't have the tools to meet those expectations, we are often disappointed. At some point, we have to take some level of responsibility and enhance our own spectrum of expectation."

Epilogue: Ten and a Half Commandments

A nature programmed to judge, shun

Have respect of persons

And, to C-L-I-Q-U-E.

System overload!

And, we wonder why

The revolving door still swings!

An inconclusive phenomenon?

Not really.

Who is to blame for unsanctified shame?

Continuously challenging converts to change

Yet, WE stay the same.

Love's requirement often unmet

Yet, we continue with business as usual.

Obliviously controlled, mesmerized

Reprobated by our own habitual ways

Yet, we debate what this all really means.

It's only a sin, if it's one of the 10!

We love because He first loved us.

Uniquely predestined to be exactly

What you were called to be.

I'm beautifully me, and you are beautifully you.

Born faulty, judgmentally defaulted
Trying to place blame on whose fault it is.
The path clearly illuminated, often interrogated
And, collaborated…AGAINST.
Defy it, turn from it, and allow it to happen.
With love and kindness, have I drawn thee?
Don't you feel it?
Step up to a higher call; hear the voice of
the Lord.
Sincerity, loyalty, vulnerability, humility.
PURE LOVE!
Uniquely predestined to be exactly what you were
called to be.
I am beautifully me and you are beautifully you!
Embellish me, entrance me, hold me close.
Love me, for real - for real.
Whisper sweet nothings in my ear.
Make me feel like a woman, a called woman.
A forgiven woman.

Freedom

"Freedom came that glorious day. It was the day I stopped seeking the validation of others, from thence forward I soared like an eagle. I had not previously known such freedom. And now, I cannot go back."

When Reality Trumps!

Your heart beating against my chest.
Your breath warm against my breasts.
The calming of your voice
Assures me that we are finally here.
Your heart beating against my chest.
Your breath warm against my breasts.
The delicate touch of your hand
Guides me to a familiar place.
Your heart beating against my chest.
Your breath warm against my breasts.
Our eyes connect bringing desire to its peak
And once again your passion has rendered me weak.
You pull me close, my face in your hands.
Over and over again.
Embellish me with your beautiful kisses.
Defenses are down, surrendered it all.
Your heart beating against my chest.
Your breath warm against my breasts.
I've metaphorically been here before
Not quite like this.
I've given in to this moment with you
And, I am here. Holistically.
Here!
And, though I've metaphorically been here before
Not quite like this.
We've transformed from the here and now to a
spiritual orbit.
Your heart is mine.
It's beating against my chest.
I am in your arms and you are in mine.
You have my heart, and I have yours.

Reject the Accuser

"Accusers of the brethren will bring false charges against individuals with the intent of weakening their influence, and injuring the cause which they are identified. The enemy is an accuser of man and he will attack your elevation and your increase. He will throw darts of confusion, calamity and destruction. Elevation requires you to reject the accuser."

The Human Experience

Often times when we are hurt by those we've let into our circle, we should bear some of the responsibility. Be a big girl and learn from those opportunities of growth. I lost two people I considered dear friends. Death didn't do us part, situations beyond repair did. One I knew I could live without, and one I never thought I'd ever have to. I put a lot into friendships, I love hard and I am loyal. When I was still growing, healing and blossoming, there was a thorn in my side who presented herself as my friend with the kiss of Judas. While I was loving, helping, and edifying; her smiles were like sharp knives. So, today, I had to be transparent and say it hurt like hell. I'm still not healed. Last night I cried. Toxicity isn't good for even the strongest of us. So, I've decided to go ahead and put it out there and heal from the outside in.

Sweet Dreams

I dreamed of a man you see

Asked God if this was the man for me

Showed me his love, gut, and his story

Shined like elements of morning glory

Revealed his love for his God

His soul, and his actions

Didn't show me his face, but showed me an extraction

Made me keenly aware of a man who'd share his life
with me

Show me his face oh Lord, let me see!

A clue, a hint, an answer, I demanded

"Not yet, you my child are not ready!"

He reprimanded

An enigma, a puzzle, paradox

Grand ole' dreams you placed in a box

Searched the face for a clue

No clues, no answers, no queues

Blurred dreams, shattered thoughts

Sleep sweet, dreams pure, love denied

For far too long, searched for things to pacify

Tragic flaws in my stars, voids in my heart

Missing clues, misinterpreting dreams

Then! Clarity came

Brought thunderous shame

Unperfected and complicated

Coherence offering vision perfected

The man in my dreams

Was the man of my dreams

Submission made easy

Loved me enough to make me a wife

Sweetly woke me up to life

Gave me the space to be

Who God clearly created me to be

Selfish clarity interrupted

The man in my dreams

Was the man of my dreams

Funny how clarity requires no human intervention.

When *Real* Transformation Begins

Some of us have such high self-esteem that we fail to
see our own flaws

No matter how amazing you are, how smart you are,
how gorgeous and how in demand you are...

Self-esteem is not enough to wipe away the crud

It is not until you look in the mirror and accept what
you see as real that you can come face to face with
who you *really* are, and work to change those things

That, my dear, is how you evolve

That, is how you grow

 And, that is the beginning of real
transformation.

Weigh it, weigh you!

'We often have the attitude that, "if I was a real friend, I'd tell them what was being said about them." We must use discretion and be careful *what* we repeat. Ask yourself, how does that negativity and damaging trash bring value to my friend's life? Most of what is said by the initiator is only said in jealousy or sheer deceit. I've sometimes heard things people have said about me, and secretly gotten mad at the person who relayed it. Thinking, how could you repeat something so horrible? Yes! We have to even be careful what we repeat to our friends. I was once a habitual gossiper, but as my life progressed I became too busy to focus on things that didn't bring me joy or stability. My life and ideals shifted. What was once important to me quickly moved into the "don't have time for that" file. We must all gain the boldness, and integrity necessary to stop bad news in its tracks; people get it when we begin to shut them down. In love, we must challenge our friends to start thinking about their life goals and their own purpose. It is my desire that we all figure that out before we leave this earth. Find out what it is that they love enough to shift their attention from idleness to healthy productivity? If we can assist in cultivating the talents and calling of someone else, we have made progress!'

Trust the Answer

"Remember that His will is perfect. He is able to do exceedingly, abundantly, above ALL that you could ever ask or think! He can do it. You must first believe with unwavering faith.
And, be prepared for His answer, His will.
Even, if the answer is no."

'I was slightly disappointed when the doctors passed me another little girl. I yearned to mother a son. When

I saw my friends with their boys, my heart instantly felt empty. I wanted a son, a male child who would love me, admire me and take care of me when I got old. God had other plans for my womb and a man child would not pass through it.

I can't imagine life without my two daughters, but the truth is I have my moments of longing. There's no other way to say it, but to say it, I've felt a void. That is, until a few months ago. I'm finally at peace knowing that it just wasn't meant to be. I could not handle the burden of giving birth to a black boy.

The turmoil, worry, and pure anxiety around mothering a black boy, and then the thought of having to bury him at the hands of consequences forced upon a people by its nation; sharing a black boy with a nation of people who are afraid of black boys would be too much for me.

And, that is just something God knew my heart couldn't handle. They say God won't put more on you than you can bear, and the recent turn of events have finally brought me closure. Mothers are grieving the deaths of their sons all over the United States, and I am grieving with them. But, I'm finally at peace knowing that I will never have to bury *my* son, or deal with the anguish of all that comes along with having a black boy pass through one's womb.'

Make your dreams come true

"As you start your week off, begin to think about what's on your to do list of goals and dreams. Take little steps toward them TODAY. Make phone calls that get you one step closer to that thing that's been tugging at your heart. Research it today. Then, manifest thoughts concerning your dreams with action until they materialize. Start today and eventually you will get there! The first step is getting your mind to do what your heart and hands already know you should be doing."

Event Cancelled!

'We have to hold our friends accountable for these witch hunts! Historically, some of us have not done that! We've sat around and had a witch hunt of sorts – in the church, among our friends, and among our colleagues.

Don't let anyone beat down another woman in your presence. Remember NO woman is your competition unless you MAKE her your competition.

How do you change a behavior that's become a ritual for women (and sometimes men)? Sometimes we don't know how the talents of others are often intertwined with how insecure we actually feel about ourselves. When we meet people we most times don't show love, we show fear and are often saturated in our assumptions. You may be asking, "how do I discontinue behavior that's become so common, so normal. So much so, that it's a part of who I am?" You stop it by starting to think about all the things that make you feel insecure. You may even realize that what you don't like about someone else is something you *love* and would actually want for yourself.'

Catch your Dream

"Move beyond coveting another's talents, gifts, beauty, and success. Figure out what you need to do to reach the goals God has established for you. Your destiny awaits you; don't get distracted along the way. Just go get YOUR dream."

"Colored Folks"

(Freestyled in the Dominican Republic in the presence of great friends)

Pinks and Blacks
Grays and blacks
Blues and blacks
All within a spectrum
Of hues and lacks
They're all here
The whole ambitious pack
Filled with dreams
They are dream chasers
Dream crushers?
Fallback!
Release the pinks and blacks
And grays and blacks
And blues and blacks
Release the blessings
Curse the spirit of lack!
The spirit that chases
The pinks and blacks
And grays and blacks
And blues and blacks
Fall back!
Release the pinks and blacks
And grays and blacks
And blues and blacks
Retract!
Move wayyyy back!

Don't Fear the Worms

"Fear is the greatest illusion ever known to mankind. Lift up your shovel's handle again and again. With all your strength, dig until fertile soil you find. Don't allow worms in the soil to determine your end. Dig for growth, dig for strength, dig for dear life."

You Have Black Friends?

My daughter was traveling this weekend with my niece and two of her friends. One of her friends are biracial and the other one is Caucasian. When my niece's suitcase was weighed at the airport counter, it weighed in at fifty pounds; she was told by the agent to lighten her suitcase or pay the fee. She pulled things out of her suitcase and shuffled stuff around to avoid the additional fee. Well, when the Caucasian friend put her suitcase up to be weighed, the ticket agent said her suitcase was overweight too, but that they could "just go". The Caucasian friend was well aware of what was happening and objected and said "so you just had her take all of her things out of her bag, but I don't have to pay?" He then began justifying his actions by stating that it had been a long day and he just didn't want to make her go through it. She challenged him and demanded he charge her the fee....even though *he wouldn't*. Even still, I salute this young woman! There is a certain awareness that comes along with actually spending time with people of color and witnessing up close and personal how we are often treated. When you see it, and stand up against bias and institutional racism, then you have a right to say I have black friends.

Better...

"There is not a love like God's! When you feel all help is gone, allow God to love you, the only way HE knows how. There is absolutely nothing in the world like a "sweet kiss" from the Lord of Lords. He will make it all better."

Death of a Thing

Think about the things you don't like about someone you know. Now, think about all the things you don't like about yourself. You can't walk into your true destiny with these "dark" things. All the things we see when we *really* look at ourselves, hold us back. You've already asked God to kill it. Countless times you have depended on him to remove the cross you bear. You asked for it to be removed, exterminated, and killed! Out of your own mouth you pleaded, "Let this cup depart from thee, Lord kill this thing, kill that thing". And the Lord is saying, "I have killed it! I killed it every time you asked me to. I killed it once, I killed it twice, three times I've killed that very dark thing that has held you hostage for far too long! But, you went and nursed it back to life! You fed it, you nurtured it, and you gave that thing life! As with a dying plant, you brought it into the light and gave it plenty of sunshine and plenty of water.

Now, that thing has grown and festered, and you are back again asking me to KILL it. All the things it needed to grow, you supplied it to that *thing*. All the things that were necessary for the survival of the thing you asked me to kill, you provided it with! The very thing that was created by the enemy to kill you has been sustained by you! You breathed LIFE back into the very thing I destroyed! Now, for the final time allow the DEATH of that thing to happen!

Mama's Baby, Daddy's maybe.

If I said I didn't care it would be a lie, if I said I never
wanted to ever see you again it couldn't be further
from the truth. Your face mirrors mine! My blood
pumps and flows red from you, but my heart
sometimes yearns the truths and love from you.
Yet, you run from your mirror's image.
How could you?
But, most of all who are you?
Lastly, where are you?

Epitome of a Dream

Time traveled deep into my dreams
Beyond a mere eye's conception
Oh, the things I envisioned!
Imagined worlds free of deception
Created nations
Exactly the way I wanted them to be
Possessed lands my heart longed to decree
Majestic mountains
And glorious seas
Wealth and grandiosity
Graciously laid at my feet
Pearls, precious jewels, and cattle
Jade-green land and houses
No worries, no fears
Fitfully fiscal
World's finest garments
Chiffons, silks
Linens and satins
Reality's chosen
Now conscious indeed
Life, health, joy, peace
The epitome of a dream.

I AM my hair

Before I knew it
I hated it!
Burned it
Permed it
Fried it
Didn't care to know it!
Bleached it
Blow dried it
Didn't want to try it
It kept coming back for more
To breathe, to be free
Growing from the roots
Curly, kinky, unfamiliar to me
Proving that I was not free
I needed to open my eyes and see
Comfortable? I'd never be
Until I allowed it to just BE
Child, I finally owned it!
Wore it
Embraced it
You don't like it?
Get over it.
This is exactly who I am with it
Without it, allowing my locks to be free
A fight would always be present
Unless I retreated and gave in
Let my hair do its own thing
Truth is opposite of what I once sang
Until, truth from my mouth rang
Former things left my soul bare
Truth is, I am…my hair.

Strong

Sometimes strong
Sometimes arrogant
Independent and humble
Sometimes weak
Sometimes dependent
Characteristics shining
Strengths dwindling
Whip me into shape, oh Lord
What am I without you?
In the dawn and at dusk
You have shown yourself strong
Your light constantly beckons me to take heed
Listen closely to your voice
And follow your creed
I am not alone
We all try to be strong
Denying our innocence
When in fact
We are all guilty of *being* stronger
Than we really are
Guilty of being arrogant and too independent
Rejecting help from the creator
Often times faltering without sound reason
We have all the power we need
But, power is often required to just lean
On the aid and assistance of something greater
One who has power
And one who is much stronger
I am nothing without you.
I am more powerful with you,
Than I could ever be alone.

Pedal to the metal

Longest shortest ride of my life
This!
This right here
Is payback for every wrong!
Every sin!
And every woman I made cry!
Every time I opened my legs to have a fetus sucked...
OUT Of my mind
I must have been crazy
Lazy
In a haze
When I chose the easy way out
Turns out...
Wasn't so easy at all!
Now....
My baby sitting next to me on the passenger side
Of my seat!
As I cried from deep down inside
Willing her to do what I didn't have the courage to do
But now I wait outside
For her fetus to be sucked
Outside...
The protestors, they got signs
They sell baby parts in there
Meanwhile I cry from deep inside...
Her precious body
My precious heritage
Medal to the pedal
No grands for me
Forget the circumstances
"She ain't married yet"
'This aint the life I chose for my baby!'

This!?
This hurts even me!
This is payback for every lie I told
Every... heart I stole
Every time I became decision maker
After I had made my choice..
Future aint' bleak
When God allowed it to be...
"Covered by your grace, no matter what I've done, no
matter where I've been, you have removed my shame,
now I am covered by your grace!"
Doors open, she steps outside
BUT I see her insides...
The look on her face
Different from the look on my face
When I took that ride
Though God will allow no shame...
Her heart...
Her heart is not broken
Her spirit remains
She's free from that pain
Not held by that stain
Or the pain...
That I felt
When I took....
The longest, shortest ride of my life.

"Cordially Invited!"

Planned a big ole' party
And everyone came
Agreed to fight injustice
And stand in the trenches
Dressed in their fancy clothes
Shiny shoes, and dresses
Celebrated and danced the night away
Unapologetically addressed our issues
High heels moved throughout the room
In a beautiful clatter
Microphone boomed
Ridding our world of this shuddering shame
"Thank you all for coming!"
But some things have got to change
Our children are hurting, our future is stuck
In an abyss, gone amuck!
Awaiting dire healing
Some were victims, some victors
Some oblivious
Never having had to deal with the pain of this disease
Nevertheless, they stood in solidarity
To fight a world of sexual injustice
To use their own power, against powers that be
And, those who destroy our young's humanity
Humanity's social justice
So desperately needed.
We are all invited to this big ole' party
Under the auspices of true, divine
Miraculous healing
To remove the elephant's freedom to roam
So, that this place we live can be called home
Because home isn't just a place

Home is a mindset, health
Spirituality and livelihood
Hold up your glasses at this national party
Feet on the ground, dance I say!
Dance, on the head of sexual injustice!
There is plenty to eat, plenty to drink, plenty to do!
We must bring justice!
Not just to us, But, to them!
And, you. And, her! And, him! And, me!
Justice to all those who just want to be free!
Dance I say, dance the night away...

#Disengage

How do you *unlove*? This may sound daunting, but I've learned how to unlove those things that have brought me continual pain. When I think about everything I truly love, those things have brought me pure joy when I've needed it most.
I find joy in only those things that feel good to my soul. Not just those things that feel good in a moment, but those things that feel good AFTER that moment has passed. When I have disengaged from those things (or persons) and I am still in a good place in my mind and in my heart I know my soul has been fed. If it doesn't feel good after you disengage you must unlove this thing. To unlove you must seek after those things that bring pure joy, long term peace and satisfaction, and those things only.

De'Vonna Pittman

"A Few Important People"

Little Girl

Let's keep quiet!

You know, like the

"Waiting in the clinic" silence!

Little girl, just hold it together.

No one can know.

They don't want the real

Only the fake.

The lies, they sound better.

They look better.

How much worse could it get for her?

Let's just walk around

Like it never happened.

Something like this should never happen!

Denial is far more pleasant than reality.

Although, we all know

This is reality.

So, just believe, that you cannot

substitute false for true

Or right from wrong.

I wonder where

The rest of the little girls have gone.

He traded his satisfaction

For her little pearls

Oh, little girl!

Little girl.

I cry for the little girl because

They will never believe her.

But, something was taken from her.

He will always have a piece

Of her mind.

Ignorance is bliss.

But, wake up and see how ignorant it is

to walk around like it never happened.

Maybe then you will see how scarred

The little girl has been.

Believe it or not it's true.

Take your head out of the clouds

because this has not been working for

you...Or us, the world!

Whether you know it or not, the little

girl is still crying.

Her insides are dying!

I'm praying for the little girls.

Oh, little girls.

Alexis Bentley

Inspiration

My inspiration is the breath in my lungs.

The limbs in my fingers, gripping my pencil.

My inspiration is the world around me.

The notebook found me, as though I was lost.

My inspiration is the soft rain violently hitting my

window, as I get tangled somewhere in my notebook.

Trying to tangle my way through my thoughts.

My inspiration is my bad days and my sad days.

Putting my heart into this

Like it's the last breath I will take.

My inspiration is my nirvana

My get away, the only way I can break away.

My inspiration is my lack of knowledge…its power.

Empty thoughts filled with thoughts about nothing

more than forty acres and a mule.

Nothingness.

My inspiration comes when I have nothing, but

Heaven's light guiding me.

Taking me to a place where no one can go but me.

My inspiration is my happiness bringing me to a

place where you can't see.

You can go there, but you can't touch me.

You feel me?

My inspiration allows my head to lay in the arms of
where my happiness brought me which is really
where my inspiration guided me.

It's our future that inspires me.

My inspiration comes from my chipped nail polish
that looks unfit, but only on the surface.

If you go deeper you can uncover hidden talents, like
when my hand takes hold of a pencil that takes hold
of paper that gets ahold of me…it's inspiring.

I am my inspiration.

Broken, ugly, beautiful, flawed, and hurt.

But, how beautiful it is to love yourself for who you
are not and who you are trying to be.

It just sounds like trying to me.

It's the thrill, and I am inspired!

Alexis Bentley

De-Ice

As we prepared to board the plane we didn't know if
we were going to be able to get on or not. Then, we
took our seats and were told that the plane couldn't
leave the runway yet.

No, not yet.

The plane needed to be "de-iced".

To wash away anything they thought would deter the
plane from getting to its destination safely, and
securely.

And, that is what God does with us.

He purges and washes us clean of anything that
might hinder us from getting to Him!

Alexis Bentley

More Insight

Inconsistency is what I was used to

I knew nothing different!

Letting him run in and out of my life

Whenever he got good and ready!

Ripping my heart to pieces

And knowing that the only comfort I had was in him.

So, I was quick to pull him right back in!

Back and forth yelling and screaming, calling me names

But at the end of the night it was okay for him to call me

baby!

Hey I was in love, I knew no other way!

Love from my mother and sister was a must

But love from a man who didn't have to love me was the

best feeling in the world!

I was high! I didn't know any better, how could you blame

me?

How naive of me to believe that a boy who didn't love

himself could love me!

I know he didn't love me

He disrespected his mother and treated her bad.

So, there is no way he could love me!

I can truly say I've loved and I've lost!

I've found myself, and I found out why I was letting these guys off the hook so easily!

It was because I let my father do the same thing

Came around when he wanted

Called when he thought it was necessary

Loved me when he didn't love himself

Then, when he was all better, it was ghost town!

He stuffed my heart with all his pain and insecurities!

Burdened with his hurt

And not capable of handling his inconsistency.

After a while it was unbearable

So, I found the only consistency I could for the moment!

I've grown since then, I've cried since then

I've hurt since then

I've hated since then

And, I've loved since then!

My latest love is a win

Because, I have found consistency for eternity

And, I found it within!

Alexis Bentley

Everlasting Heartbreak

A smile turned into a frown
What's a daughter without a dad?
Who can I run to?
An uncle who has a family of his own
My chest is aching, my feet are tired
I looked low, I looked high

Alexis Bentley

Closed for Business

You cuddled with me
Like I was the last pillow
You would ever grab hold of
You dropped me off
Like you never wanted to say goodbye
But you never called back
Until the next night
And I will never know why
It happened again
On my body you depend
I am more than a late night creep
Not a backdoor freak
Or any other thing I allowed you to reduce me to
Filling me up with the love you've never had
And will never have with me
Every day I fight myself trying to let you go
At night you bring my body pleasure, but by day you
bring my mind pain
I feel like the abandoned child that no one wanted to
care for but wanted to get bare for
Well I am done laying down
It's time for me get up
To stand up and stop giving up what was so
preciously given to me
I AM DONE

Alexis Bentley

The Roots of Me

I am from the project floors of Ford Heights, Illinois,
From Tussin in the dollar store and the candy store in
Mrs. Virge's house. I am from the big, somebody-
punched-a hole-in-the-wall, type projects.

I am from "The Golf Course of Chicago Heights,"
where our family hosts our family reunion, from Big
Mama Lucinda and Big Daddy Henry and "The
Bentleys".

I am from the daddies leaving their kids because they
are deadbeat and single mothers deserving respect
because they worked their butts off to raise those
kids' type projects.

I am from the "girl, wake up and clean your room
before I get that belt" type projects.
From Granny whippin Mama because she snuck out,
and Big Mama asking my mom and aunts to spend
the night because she wanted them to clean her house
type projects.

I am from the vinegar Auntie Edna Mae used to clean
the stained stairs with. I remember the parties, and
the pickles that my momma, my aunts, and uncles
used to stick a peppermint in just to suck out all the
pickle juice kind of projects. Where they ate collard
greens with hot sauce and pig feet with mustard in
those projects.
I am the picture in the shoe box that mama filled up
with family memories of a lifetime, but I am distinctly
from my grandmother, Dorothy!

I was born in Minneapolis, Minnesota, but I am from
the poor city of Ford Heights, Illinois. By way of the
deep hot south of Greenville, Mississippi.
I was born and bred from the struggles of the projects.
A home filled with love, type of projects.
That, is where I am from.

Alexis Bentley

ℒetter to My Mother

So many years, and so many words

The love between us, and secrets it holds

So much for me, you have always provided

Years have passed, and now it's time to write it

You are the queen of queens

My queen of queens you have saved me

No words can describe how you have changed me,
my life

Always willing to give and sacrifice everything for
little ole' me

Sometimes I couldn't understand how you held so
strong

Though the odds were against you, you held on so
long

Sometimes I think God sent you, his most beautiful
angel here just to save me

So, I weep with joy in my heart

You are my heart, the only light that leads me out of
the dark

You are my get away, the only way I can break away, is in your arms

You are my sunshine, my only sunshine, you make me happy when skies are gray

All those dark nights when all you could do was pray

Oh, how I thank God for gracing me with you, such a mother

There is no other, like YOU!

You are unique and hand-made piece by piece

And they tried to tear you apart piece by piece

Little by little they tried to make you so much smaller

But it only made you that much taller...

He sent you to do it

Because he knew that you could do it

For all those who didn't do it,

You are the living proof

For all those who didn't think you could do it.

You are God's gift to the world and you have always been

But you are just now starting to release yourself from the box he so carefully placed you in

It's time to unwrap, unwrap yourself from the pain,
unwrap yourself from the shame

I promise to help you throw the wrapping paper
away

This is just the beginning and you have so much to
gain

Release your story to the world; let your light shine
on the world

And in doing so I will be right beside you

You should never have any doubts if you believe in
yourself like I believe in you.

Alexis Bentley

Nervous

Why am I so nervous?
Why am I so nervous!
I step on the stage praying for acceptance
No aggressions, just fear....
I am afraid
Once again I ask myself again why I am so nervous!
I come from a people who fought
They were never afraid or nervous
But, this stage I can't seem to own
I can't make it mine....
Possessions?
I am possessed with a spirit of fear
Even though I come from a God who said, my dear as
long as you hold me near, I will help thee!
Releasing myself to world
I live in a world that will scare you!
I am afraid of what the world has to offer
Deal or no deal! I am playing myself, selling myself
short....
So again I ask myself why am I so nervous?
I am my own worst critic
The world can't criticize me, because I have already
done that to myself, me!
What do I stand for? What do I stand on?
My platform is scary
You couldn't dare me to stand on it
No power
But if knowledge is power, why does it taste so sour
These words I can't seem to devour
One big gulp of fear, but it just won't seem to go
down
These nerves are keeping me bound

Feet still on the ground, no height in sight,
Gravity is working, holding me back
Why the hell am I so nervous to go out and achieve
the world, live life? To take flight?
I wanna take off, but I can't because I'm just way to
nervous!
And, I'm still asking myself...why?
Am I afraid of what people may think or am I afraid
of me?

Alexis Bentley

Not picture perfect, but me

If you look at me you see the slanted eyes of Sonny
The round nose from Devonna Pittman
And lips that come from God knows where
You will see a girl with a chocolate face, and high
cheekbones
But if you look a layer deeper…
You will see the cheekbones that hurt from smiling
Ribs that became sore from laughing at the funny
movie "Super Bad"
You will see a temple that belongs to God
You will see a heart that is broken from all the
negativity that surrounds me
But you will also see determination
That comes from my strong beautiful mother
You will encounter my soul that sings beautiful music
And, shy away from darkness
If you look in my spirit, you will see
A girl who longs for her best friend
because she has moved away
And muscles that ache from the bat coming in contact
will the ball that will end in a homerun
A layer deeper…..
And you are back to the surface

Alexis Bentley

"My pretty & Its Ugly Truth"

I am pretty, oh so pretty
I'm pretty and witty
Who is that?
What is she wearing?
Girl, this is school....not a fashion show
Does she have on lipstick?
Like, come on we're in class, not the club
This is what I do
This is what I have to do; this is all the stuff I go
through
You know, lying to save face, although I must admit I
am not in a pretty state
Long hair don't care, head held in the air
Just to keep the tears from falling
Hitting the ground, I have begun to sink...
I don't wanna think, feel, or hurt
Look at me, I am pretty...oh, so pretty
Now look at me again...
Can't you see the disguise?
Look past my smile, my eyes.
...anything that is physical
You know they say, "never let em' see
you sweat"
You always want them to think you're a threat
So, I traded my tears for a pretend smile
My laughter for a pretend show
My hurt for happiness and my pain
You see, I hold that deep down in my veins
Pushed it to the back of my brain
None were in sight, now look at me again, you see
this right here?
This is me and I am giving me to you

Take me in, breathe ME, because this is the only way you will understand me
I need you to know how It feels to be me, hold me
I carry the weight of world on my back, in my stomach
I just can't run from it, I wanna escape it but I can't
So, I just embrace it
My healing phase, it's more of a process.
Something you cannot process, you couldn't even begin to image
Imagine me broken down, beat up, torn up and worn out
Now look at me one more time
This is me patching up old wounds and covering old scars.
Trying to forgive
Trying to love
Trying to move forward, while continuing to look above
So when you see me, understand this one thing
I am a work in progress, trying to maintain on this journey throughout my healing process

Alexis Bentley

Sorry, and...

I'm sorry that you have to live with your regret.

I'm sorry that you have to sleep in your regrets.

I'm sorry that you have to wake up in the middle of
the night and look at your regret as a result of what
you failed to do.

I'm sorry that you have to drunk-text me to find peace
in the midst of your regret.

I'm sorry that you wake up every morning just to
remember your regrets.

I'm the kind of girl God gives you
young, so you'll know loss for the rest of
your life. So, I'm sorry that you have to
settle to calm the storm of your regrets. I'm sorry that
regret will consume you
until you are covered and you can no longer stand it.

I bid you farewell, and I'm sorry for your regrets.

I wonder if you're sorry now.

Alexis Bentley

Young, Fabulous and Brokenhearted

I am scared, ok
Never have I felt so strongly
So quickly
You are the characteristics I put in my bible for only
God to read
You are my deepest and most urgent need
I can feel the love you're capable of, and it's all too
real
It possesses the power to heal my deepest wound
I am afraid I won't have you forever
That this can't be a happily ever after, because life
isn't a movie, right?
I am confused
Working slowly toward a "we"
But you haven't moved on from her
You better recognize
Real eyes
I realized
Why I can't be the winner
Cause I'm not trying
Crying because I'm afraid of firsts
Who took away my champion?
Made me forget I can move mountains
I am my worst nightmare
Worst
Nightmare
That's why
I am scared, ok!

Teiara Hayslett

Caution

I was warned this could be dangerous
Look at me now
Just waiting
Sitting
Mind racing
But still, I'm just waiting
Just wanna hear your voice or receive your text
Contemplating
I just really wanna be your next
But, I'm still just waiting
Because I know it's not time yet
We still got some growing to do
Just hoping
Mind floating
But I'm still just hoping
Dreaming, wanting, breathing
Dreaming, wanting, waiting
Hoping
While he's sleeping on me, and in his dreams laying
with she
Really? I just wanna wrap my leg around you and
hold you tight
Pull you in close and kiss you slow
I just wanna cherish these last few moments
Hurting...
Knowing...
I graduated and moved away
We'll never happen again
I just wanna tell you that I think I could love you
better
Not better than her, just better than you have ever felt
before

I just wanna have you next to me forever
But, I know that's too much to ask
I just wanna be your forever
I don't want you to just "take my friendship to the
moon and back"
I want you to have my love right here on this earth
I just wanna....
Go to sleep and not wonder how you feel about me.

Teiara Hayslett

Never say never

I hate you and your species.
Is that poetic enough for you??
It's just that simple.
No need to use metaphors
Or to say it in a poetic tone.
Two times, say it two times, broken two times
All from two lines.
You wanna know why I still talk to you?
It's because I "can never give my all to anything".
That's what the new guy said.
What a waste of my time.
Why am I wasting my mind, body and soul on this again?
Chasing him, he's chasing her, "I'm in loooovee with another woman".
And
"I'm sorry - I'm so sorry!"
Stop right there!
There goes that feeling again.
Heart racing
Heart-breaking feeling again.
I hate you, but don't worry you weren't the first guy.
It's been done before you by another *good* guy.
Soooo, I've heard it all before and it hurts less every time.
And I know it wasn't on purpose, but I hate you and I hate him.
I hate all the time we spent
All the times I vented
All the love I lent.
And I'm soooo drained.
I hate you!

Never again.
I remember how I felt on this day.
Felt myself slowly drifting away.
Away with the wind cause that's what I feel.
Sitting on the sidewalk,
Real, real close to the ground,
But then I found Passion...

Teiara Hayslett

Passionate

Find inspiration
Picture it
Draw it
Sew it
Hem it
Sell it
I'm a changed woman and now my smile is so big
That river I cried dried up
And I must admit I'm flattered
You texted that you miss me
They say you never know what you got until it's gone
And baby
I'm gone...
Growing Always

Teiara Hayslett

Follow me as I follow Christ

It is very hard to keep up with me

Path paved long time ago

Been walking in and on it for quite some time

The foolish only inquire and ponder on how to
follow, but the wise pay attention and get in step.

In doing so, you have to have endurance

Baby, I am one TOUGH cookie

And, not to mention, I'm a resilient woman

Pushing forward has never been an opposition

Mighty trials conquered by a mighty God's will

Tiffany Washington

Losing her balance

As she sits behind a broken door
Her eyes are bloodshot red
And, her tears are dropping to the floor
She ponders on her past
Wondering why her angels couldn't last?
Fixed smiles for the pictures, ready, set, flash
But she's your little girl right?
You would give her the world right?
But you let her out of your sight
Alcohol and cocaine blurred your eyes
Now, there are screams through the house and the
little girl is forced to fight
Blood begins to soak through the carpet and her mom
is crying in her lap
What 13-year-old should have to go through that?
After that her soul begin to face a challenge
Who is she?
Beginning to lose her balance
She's slipping through life
Finding love in a knife
She's fighting an addiction
Trying to sort through real love and fiction
Mama you're sick
She knows it's not your fault
She got scars you could have noticed…
But, she tried to show it
She still losing her balance, can't anyone tell?
Her name is Deja Patricia Norris
Period.
And don't forget Wells
Deja Patricia Norris

Grandma,

There are so many things that I want to tell you, I don't even know where to begin. I guess I'll start by thanking you for being the BEST grandmother anybody could have. Although you were my grandmother, you were more like my mom. I don't know if you realize this, but out of my thirty-seven years here on this earth, I've only been away from you for four of them, which was when I moved to Georgia with mom. Thank you for the things you've taught me. I was telling a friend a couple of weeks ago that one of my biggest fears was that if you died and if I were to forget something you taught me, that you wouldn't be around for me to ask. Their response was that "you won't forget what she has taught you, because it's instilled in you and that's what makes you the woman you are today." And although I know that, I'm still afraid because you were still teaching me things up until the day you passed away. So, who am I going to ask now? The one thing I know I'm not going to forget is how you taught all of your children to be kind to people and how to treat them. You would say, "Those same folks you treat badly might be the ones you need to get a piece of bread from." You were full of anecdotes.

You also taught us how to love. You had so much love in your heart for your children, and people in general. Your love was unconditional and you have taken care of a lot of folks!! You have listened, gave me your thoughts, and said, "you know I'm here for you if you need me," and I truly appreciate that.

And, I'll go ahead and tell you this too, your grandson was coming to visit as well. I told Chris on Wednesday, "Grandma is going to be full of surprises tomorrow". But, we were the ones to get the surprise.

Around 3:20 A.M. on Thursday morning, Rita called to tell me that the nurse advised her to call the family because they weren't sure you were going to make it through the night, and at 3:50 A.M., GOD called you home. I was ten minutes too late to see you off. You lived your life as a true born again Christian. You've often told me that if you didn't tell me anything else, the one thing that you will say is to get my life right with the LORD, so that I can go to heaven. I know that I'm not where I need to be with the LORD, but I will get there so that I can see you again. Grandma, I am going to miss you dearly... words can't even express. I will ALWAYS love you and you will ALWAYS be in my heart, and you will NEVER be forgotten. Just know that I will take care of Ciara and Christopher as you have taken care of me. And, as I told you on Thursday, I'm not going to say goodbye, I'm going to say, see you later.

With all my love,

Roshonda Royston (Your oldest grandchild)

This letter was originally written on June 17, 2012, in memory of Deloris (Rayford) Falks

Fearfully and Wonderfully Made

Fearfully and wonderfully made, that's me you see.
So comfortable in my skin that you would never
understand.
From my head to my feet, what you see is what you
get. Best believe that this is NOT a test.
Every hair on my head has been accounted for, so
there's no need for you to try and explore.
Eyes of golden brown that would win any stare
down.
A nose that permeates no matter what the reason.
Just know that who I am is always in season.
Fearfully and wonderfully made, that's me you see
Lips lavishly sweet, luscious and seductive
They can either build you up or prove to be
destructive.
Shoulders broad enough to carry life's
burdens
Remembering that each one serves a purpose
The stride in my steps are confident
And, with poise - as I'm guided by MY inner voice
The sway in my hips and the rumble in my thighs lets
everyone know YES SHE HAS ARRIVED!
Fearfully and wonderfully made, that's me you see
The thickness of your lips
And the width of your hips will always be a
discussion
Know who you are
And, let them harvest the repercussions
Your negative comments....
Don't bother

For you see I am the work of the Father
Created in His image and nothing less
I am a queen and require only the best
Bone of my bone and flesh of my flesh
Here I stand, so you know the rest!

LaToya Wilson

No one shall ever believe that sanitizing & spreading

Icing on cold, hard stones would render them fit to

serve as

Gastronomic delights — warmly received & gingerly

digested at the table of

Good intentions set to satisfy even the greatest desires

Emanating from the fiercest hunger to

Right repeatedly-dished out wrongs — so RIP, n-word.

WINDOWPAIN

On the other side, the grass is greener
The sun is shining, the air is cleaner
On the other side, I can see clearly
All my dreams
Some constantly deferring
What is this existence, I chose to live
Blindly
But, on purpose
Disintegrating to fear
I try to sleep peacefully
But, I'm constantly awake
Looking straight in the mirror at illogical fate
I believed I had no power to change my condition
No power to move
Or escape my crippling disposition
What was this imagery that revealed lies told?
Making me believe that love should be cold
Emotional abuse so cunningly sweet
Smiling and lip syncing
With purpose of defeat
I supported the facade of a false reality
Not realizing at first that the joke was on me
Darkness eclipsed, damaging my leaves
Crushing, destroying and burying my seed
Finally the heavens have opened with light
Patented by my creator and protected by right
There is no fear in perfect love
Those are God's words
Written from above
So....
Now, I am free from *window-pain*
All things have become new
I can see again....

Nesey Davis

Vertical Affinity

I,

Limited to this rhetorical rendering,
Observe a gravity,
Viciously frightening to this point,
Every ounce of my soul is being pulled,

Yelling a quiet surrender,
Oblivion is too many syllables spilled,
Understanding sweet silence,

Slaves have never known better chains,
Or the beauty of this bondage,

Man-kind has not been,
Using roses to adorn,
Churches filled with empty pews,
How many have sat full of self without.

Pierre Fulford

Comparisons...Epiphany

Knew your heart when we started
You drowned from a love
Left broken-hearted
Still entangled in her lover's web
Distorted your view
Tried to recreate what was
"And let me start with you."
I fell in line
Thought all could be sublime...in the beginning
Tightness of my feet in those shoes
Soon had an ending
Got caught up in a sea of
"This is how I want *YOU* to be."
Not fully understanding the plight of
Comparisons...Epiphany
Trust, we're not the same
See me, see her
The past is to blame
Love can't compete
Comparisons...Epiphany
I was no Angel, caught in my own fight
Battling the past myself
Not over those loves who didn't do right
Upper-cut, left hook...
Straight bobbing & weaving
Past knocked me out and won
Now...*who* did the deceiving?
Yet you're not them...
And they're not you
My hardened heart was locked and bolted
Too much to break through
Male image I see
Felt all would wrong me

Guess we're both playing this game of
Comparisons...Epiphany
Trust, they're not the same
See you
See them
The past is to blame
Love can't compete
Comparisons...Epiphany

Tara Stone

Faith to Forgive

Will you ever forgive?

Will you ever just let go and live?

Will you ever be free?

Will you ever decide to unravel the chains on your mind

and see…differently?

Yes, it happened…no, it wasn't right

It could've still happened had you put up a fight

Regardless of the could'ves, should'ves,

Whats, whens or whys

The only thing that's got you trapped now is

The deceit from the devil's lies

See, a seed was planted in the heart

So, so long ago

And turned into a big ole' tree,

And clogged God's overflow…with its roots

Of bitterness and all those festering strange fruits

Shame, guilt, anger, depression

Envy, jealousy, rivalry, and suppression

Ah, there's just so many!!…I dare not even repeat

This fruit ain't worthy of nothing at all

And CERTAINLY not good to eat

So, it's time

Oh yes, it's time, my beautiful friend

To choke it up and let it go

An abundant life's waiting

If you send, all your cares to the Father
Who knows you best
Have Faith to forgive and uproot that nasty tree
And be assured, He'll handle the rest
Everything happens for a reason and in its season
God don't throw on you more than you can bear
Though the tragedy feels like your life committed treason
Keep believin' and don't try to get even
Just be still…and work on YOU
Allow the Almighty's blood to cleanse your heart
And plant His Love anew
By the Power of the Holy Ghost!
Be healed, transformed and walk in liberty
Have the Faith to forgive
In vibrant newness, boldly live
So they can see, internal reflections of glory
Changing your destiny
From death to life abundantly.

Tara Stone

The Man
(Dedicated to the man who desires change and a second chance)

He was sitting and thinking about a probable cause
Because you probably did not believe
He could make it.
The bars were home for most nights
Relationships were built off of "my bruh" fights.
Temptation was no longer temptation
As it became first nature
And so on and so on, his sad song.
How long shall you live in contempt?
And will you even attempt to be the man
That not only your father would scold
But the man your mother would hold?
Silent tears at night
When apparently men do not cry, that's a lie!
Most cry and die inside and we ask society why?
No particular reason at all
Just an assumption that "the man" would fall.
While standing on broken feet, "the man's" evil fans
Proclaimed him successor of defeat.
Not knowing that love would start showing,
encouraging "the man" to keep going.
In spite of failed trys and the coming and going in
and out of the home.
No doubt your child may question,
"Daddy what you gonna do?"
In spite of losing a good job
Making good money, albeit your change got strange
And you still lost your honey.
The man takes off his mask in the "he-man" parade
Decides to march on in his journey
Without any accolade.
The jail is no longer an option
Perhaps a quiet moment with a book in the library

Reminiscing on all of his earned camaraderie.
The man with the plan will stand holding up his hand
To the man that died to make him free.
Opinions no longer matter
It's not about you or me.
The man realizes every shot is worth three, not two.
He's won the game he was playing is now done.
While these feet of brokenness are now healing
And, the bruises of circumstance are fading away.
The man looks to heaven and thanks God
For giving him a new day.
He was sitting and thinking about a probable cause,
Because he knew you probably would say,
"It's a new day."
Is that really *the man*?

Elizabeth Bratton
(aka) Eladywriter

Alto Woes

It's hard being an Alto
When you're singing in the choir
You see, sopranos can hit those high notes
That all the people admire
The bass booms like thunder
The tenors can sing a strong melody
But the Altos part is on two notes
Or if we're lucky, maybe three
Now it doesn't matter what we sing, from hymn
books or acapella
Our director can gives us that look
Or sometimes he may holla
Too high, too low
Too fast, too slow
You're holding that note too long
No matter how hard we try
We still get it wrong
So shed a little tear for the Altos
One thing that we know
In the ranks of choral singers
We're considered kinda low
Now Altos can be so very humble - that a lot of
people forget em'
They'd love to sing soprano, but their vocal cords
won't let em'
But one thing is for sure
When the final trumpet sounds
And the dead in Christ shall rise
We'll all come together in that heavenly choir,
And sweetly harmonize!

Wanda L. Baker

Happy Father's Day, Dad
(To Robert Pittman, Father's Day 2015)

"I'm in the store writing this, so I promise it's not going to be too long. Actually, I'm not writing it, I'm speaking into my phone. I could go on and on about everything we've been through and all that's brought us to this place we're at now. There were times we've argued and gone back and forth and didn't see eye to eye. It's so crazy when I think of how long it took us to get here. But, we've finally arrived! And, I can't even remember the exact point in my life where I thought to myself this man is my *father*.

I know you provided so much, but I was still missing that fatherly love. I needed that, coming-to-all-of-my-dances, kind of love. That, tucking-me-into-bed, kind of love. That hugging-and-holding-me-and-giving-me-a-kiss-on-my-forehead, kind of love. Honestly, I think there was *so much* that I felt I needed from you growing up. Now, as a grown woman, I wonder if I didn't allow you to love me like that. Now, that we've *arrived*, I hope I do now, because I love you like I am your only child.

Your blood doesn't run through my veins, but I'm a Pittman in every way. I am yours. Not only have you watched me grow as a person, but you've seen me evolve as a woman. And, I've watched you grow too; you've become kind, selfless, loving, thoughtful, lenient, and considerate - and, you've become a cool dude.

We are so much alike in ways that don't even make sense to me. Now, we can still get on each other's nerves, but we love each other so hard that regardless of what we go through we're good, because we're family! Thank you for being the best provider and father that any woman could ever have.

This wasn't the typical Father's Day spiel, but you know me, I'm just keeping it real. I love you with all my heart. Don't stop being you. I love you just the way you are."

Brittany Bentley

The Vision

There they were
Lining the long moth green hallway
In the office complex across the street
It appeared to be hundreds of them
Beckoning for us and crying "Help us!"
Sitting and reaching out for my assistance
Grabbing for *my* immediate attention
God please silent their cries and hide their faces
The cries of anguish and faces of distress are too
overwhelming for me
When at last
I reached my destination down the hall
I looked back only to find the hallway empty
I can no longer hide behind the wall of ignorance
And pretend I did not hear the call
I will answer
But, not today...
Perhaps tomorrow

Cheryl Bogan

Let me think about how I want to say this, so you really get it. I've sorta been thinking about it since about 6 am. It was one of those thoughts that has lingered since yesterday. The way it layered itself in my brain as an unfinished thought, left me sort of paralyzed. I'm sure when I finally grasp its full conception it will sound different, and it will certainly feel different. Regardless, it has inspired me to write. Not many things do that. For now it's more like a half thought and a premature contemplation of many ideas and opinions. Sit down, pull up a chair and hold the napkin horizontally in mid-air, hands read to drop, right on your lap...but wait! There are always two sides to a story, not three mainly two. Your version based on your perceptions, and her version based on her own perceptions. So, before you take a side clear your head. Begin with the purest of intention, gather the facts, and then gather you! Gather up ALL of who you are, all that most people don't know about you, those dirty, judgmental, perverted thoughts, bring it all to the table. If you have been able to live with who you are, you can surely live with who you assume others to be. Now, with the purest of intentions straighten your shoulders, clear your throat, and let the napkin fall. Sit straight up in your chair, now...let's have the conversation, but only if it's going to make us all better people."

De'Vonna Pittman

What are you really made of?

When a person finds their passion NOTHING can stop them. There's no time to talk, only to do what their soul is calling them to do. When your soul calls you to do something, you do it! Difference between talkers and doers is while the talkers are talking the doers are WINNING. What are you made of though? How long have you been whining, codependent, making excuses, blaming, angry, lacking ambition, making up scenarios in your head to fit the black hole you're in? What are you really made of? Baby, honey-child...that which you are made of will continually be left in the dust, unless you become a doer and not just a talker. Lastly, at some point doers get tired of hearing hot air from talkers....show us what you're made of. Show YOU what you're made of!

De'Vonna Pittman

The Power of Love and Pain

On Thursday night my daughter was summoned to the hospital to be induced. We were thinking we'd have a baby by at least the wee hours of Friday morning. The calls were coming in from all across the country, "Is he here yet????" Nope. She was still in labor.

My daughter Alexis was in labor for 3 days! She decided on natural birth and no drugs, and she stuck to the birth plan for her child for three whole days. Between one and two hour naps we walked the halls with her for 36 hours while she was in excruciating pain.

It was one of the hardest things for me as a mother to watch. A baby being born...that happens every day, but what I experienced watching my child, my baby experience was surreal. My daughter hadn't verbally said a word for three days, because she was in THAT much pain.

And, then...In the most precious moment of alone time, I coached her into having a conversation with her baby boy Bentley, as she had done every day since finding out she was pregnant. She said, mom it hurts too much to talk. "I know baby, but he hasn't heard your voice, he needs to hear you." And then in the strongest and most audible voice...followed the sweetest words ever heard..."Bentley, I love you. We all love you. We are here...waiting for you...your family is here. C'mon BABY, just get here and I will do the rest. I love you Bentley!"

And we wept together silently. I knew Bentley heard her voice.

Later that afternoon the doctor, "you're not dilating more than four centimeters, and the baby's heart rate is dropping, you should consider a C-section." As much as she wanted to have a "natural birth," she loved her son more than a birth plan. And with the support of her family and her doula, she and Brandon agreed to an epidural and a C-section.

My grandson Bentley Brandon McIntyre was born one hour later, on Saturday, September 23 at 2:45 pm, but not until after the doctors released the chord that was wrapped around his neck. Bentley was face up. He was not coming into this world unless they went in to get him.

I believe he spoke into Alexis's heart and said, "I hear you mama and I believe you, but I need you more than you need me."

Bentley made us stronger, he made us happier, and my life will never be the same. The strength and courage my daughter exhibited made me proud to say I am her mother.

Alexis, I am so proud of you. Congrats to you and Brandon. Thank you for my grandson.

About the Contributors

Alexis Bentley is a published poet, and loves the power of words. She is a recent graduate of Eastern Illinois State University. Alexis majored in Mass Communications and Broadcast news. She represented Minnesota in 2015 for national title of Miss Black US Ambassador.

Teiara Hayslett is a recent graduate of Illinois State University. She majored in Family and Consumer Sciences with a concentration in apparel merchandising. She is currently in the process of creating her own clothing line.

Tiffany Washington is a mother, grandmother, friend, and a woman of many talents; she is an event planner, creative consultant, and a personal stylist.

Roshonda Royston is following in her grandmother's footsteps by taking on the role of humanitarian. She is a graduate of Metropolitan State University with a Bachelor's in Business Administration and is currently pursuing her Master's in Public Administration. Roshonda lives in Minnesota with her husband and their two children.

Deja Patricia Norris is a recent high school graduate who plans to study dentistry in the fall. She discovered her love for writing many years ago. She is continuously inspired by her dear departed mother.

LaToya Wilson is a God fearing mother, wife, Nana, mentor, educator, lyricist and inspirational speaker. She's been employed in Corrections for over 10 years, and is an instructor of higher education.

Iris Formey Dawson, Four years at Princeton polished Iris's skills; but growing up in Savannah, Georgia, in a household of great expectations laid her foundation. Known as The Word Sculptor, this poet, author, and editing coach has had pieces published in Essence magazine and the Encyclopedia of the Harlem Renaissance. Twitter: @thewordsculptor.

Nesey Davis is an anointed soloist, who uses her voice to bring healing to the masses. She is undeniably an incredible vocal powerhouse, originally hailing from East St. Louis, IL. For years she's traveled the nation spreading the gospel with soul and grace. She also provided lead vocals on the hit single "It's My Time" from the Grammy nominated artist Excelsior's "Soul Interpretations." She's currently working on her sophomore project due out early spring 2016.

Pierre Fulford is a Poet for the people. Follower of Jesus. To see the world put "Two in the Air" is the peaceful mission.

Tara Stone is a daughter, sister, mother, friend, writer, singer, songwriter, entrepreneur and child of God. She is the founder of "GOD OUT OF THE BOX *Conversations*" (formally *Coffee & Conversations*) where real life topics are discussed in an authentic, "real talk" fashion, from a believer's perspective. Tara's ability to think innovatively, coupled with a creative and energetic personality (and checkered past) pushes her to utilize her gifts to spread God's message of healing and love through relationship with Him.

Wanda Baker lives in Flint, Michigan and has been writing poetry for many years. She sings in her church choir and loves the Lord.

Elizabeth Bratton (Eladywriter) is a writer by nature, and has written and produced numerous Gospel plays. She is the author of the CD titled "Spoken to the Woman". Elizabeth is in the final stages of her first book a Christian novel, and she acknowledges God for her talent.

Brittany Bentley is a graduate of Grambling State University in Louisiana, she is currently teaching 3rd grade boys. She love teaching children and watching them transform from the beginning to the end of the school year. She attends the University of Minnesota and is pursuing a Master's degree in Education.

Cheyrl Bogan serves as the president and founder of Women in Ministry Fellowship International. This ministry focuses on encouraging women who minister in the Kingdom of God. This ministry has allowed her to travel and minister aboard. Cheryl has a passion to see women reach their full potential in the Kingdom of God. She is a licensed Evangelist and member of Emmanuel Tabernacle COGIC. Currently, she is finishing her Master Degree in Organizational Management from Concordia University. She enjoys, writing, traveling, learning about other cultures.

About De'Vonna Pittman

De'Vonna Bentley-Pittman is an author, blogger, and international public speaker. She has a passion for community engagement and believes in mentoring emerging leaders and professionals.

In 2012, Mrs. Pittman released her memoir "My Pretty and Its Ugly Truth," her story of overcoming poverty and abuse. She is committed to providing leadership and training to end the sexual exploitation of young girls and boys and uses her memoir as a tool to bring continued awareness to these issues.

As a former Board Member of the Sexual Violence Center in Minneapolis, Minnesota, Mrs. Pittman continues to play a very active role within the organization and lends her philanthropic efforts by supporting the very survival of the organization.

She has two novels in the que and is in the process of writing a self-help book. She lives in Minneapolis, Minnesota, with her husband and enjoys spending time with her two adult daughters.

Made in the USA
Middletown, DE
16 February 2019